GRANDPARENTS

Gifts of Love, Humor, and Wisdom

GRANDPARENTS
Gifts of Love, Humor, and Wisdom

Carolyn J. Booth and Mindy B. Henderson

RUTLEDGE HILL PRESS®

Nashville, Tennessee

A Thomas Nelson Company

Published by Rutledge Hill Press, a Thomas Nelson Company, P.O. Box 141000, Nashville, Tennessee 37214.

Photographs on pages 10 and 16 © by Jean-Claude Lejeune and used by permission. Photograph on page 93 © by Jim Whitmer and used by permission. Photograph on page 38 © by Alden A. Lockridge and used by permission. Photograph on page 139 © Chris Hodge and used by permission. Photograph on page 223 courtesy of Bryan Curtis. All other photographs courtesy of the authors.

Library of Congress Cataloging-in-Publication Data

Booth, Carolyn J., 1938–
   Grandparents : gifts of love, humor, and wisdom / Carolyn J. Booth and Mindy B. Henderson.
     p. cm.
   ISBN 1-55853-851-8
    1. Grandparents—Quotations, maxims, etc. I. Henderson, Mindy B., 1960– II. Title.

       PN6084.G6 B66 2000
       306.874'5—dc21

                                          00-046006

Printed in the United States of America

1 2 3 4 5 6 7 8 9—05 04 03 02 01 00

To my grandparents John Wilburn and Viola Jenkins, "Granddaddy and Grandmother Jenkins," and Dudley and Hilda Booth, "Daddy Booth and Granny," who raised the wonderful children that became my parents. To David and Carolyn Booth, "Pa Pa and Mom Mom," and Edward and Mildred Henderson, "Papa and Grandma," who are the most loving supportive grandparents in the world to my children, Jared and Jessica. God has blessed my family through the lives of these eight wonderful people.

INTRODUCTION

Generations come and generations go. With each generation grandparents may look different, dress different or have different roles in their grandchildren's lives. One thing that remains unchanged, however, is the deep love grandparents and grandchildren share for each other.

The look and smile on a grandchild's face as he/she anticipates an outing with you, or spots you in the crowd at a ball game, school play, music recital, grandparents day at school, or maybe even at his/her wedding is a joy and a thrill for a grandparent that money cannot buy. That look on your grandchild's face says "love," and you know you are special in that child's life. This book includes stories and sayings from Rutledge Hill Press's grandparents book collection: *Grandmother by Another Name*, *Grandfather by Another Name*, *I Love My Grandmother Because . . .*, and *I Love*

My Gandfather Because . . . . They convey the love that grandparents and grandchildren have for each other and the names that grandchildren call their grandparents.

Grandparents add a special richness to a child's life like no one else. If you are a grandparent, give your grandchildren what they long for most—your time. Read to them, rock and sing to them, play with them, attend their special activities, take them on trips, encourage them, listen and talk to them, and teach them to pray and to know God. The greatest inheritance you can leave them is a part of your heart given with time and unconditional love. You never know when you are making a memory, so make the most of every day.

—*Carolyn*

GRANDPARENTS

Gifts of Love, Humor, and Wisdom

Children's children are a crown to the aged.

—Proverbs 17:6

Grandchildren learn by experience. I had often told my grandson that my grandfather and I loved to fish together. When he turned five years old, I took him out on my farm to the pond. We sat together, silently, with our hooks in the water. He squirmed a little, as if he were getting bored. Suddenly, his line pulled a bit, and he looked at me and said, "Grandpa, I got a bite!"

He and I reeled the fish in. As I took it off the hook, I knelt to show him his catch. He was grinning ear to ear and then his eyes met mine. There we were grandfather—grandson. A feeling fell over me at that instant, because I knew that suddenly he had experienced it. The love of fishing with his grandfather—a love that would be passed on to my great-grandchildren.

If you want good advice, consult an old man.

—Romanian Proverb

I LOVE MY *Grandfather* BECAUSE . . .

He pushes me as high as the sky on my swing.

∞

Every Saturday we go someplace special.

He helps me with my homework.

He taught me to make model airplanes.

I know he loves me.

I LOVE MY *Grandmother* BECAUSE . . .

She makes me feel important.

∞

We have family hugs with her and Pop.

She puts magic cream on my boo-boos
and makes the hurt go away.

She makes yummy chocolate gravy!

She taught me to follow my heart.

Being a grandmother ranks right up there with becoming a mother, only more fun and less work!

One day my daughter ran into my mother's house and yelled, "Let me see it!"

"What?" asked my mother.

"Your Grammy Award! You must have one!"

My mother beamed. She looked at me and then gave my daughter the biggest hug. "That's just for people in the music business, sweetie!"

"Well, you should have one, too," protested my daughter. "No one deserves a Grammy Award more than my grammy!"

Grammie

One Halloween night, I opened the door to the most adorable little three- or four-your-old spook. He asked me if I had any children. I told him, "I have big children, but my daughter will soon be having a baby."

On hearing my good news, this precious little child dropped his bag of treats, put both hands to his face, looked at me with big eyes filled with more love than you can imagine, and exclaimed, "You're going to be a Grammie?"

I knew then I wanted to be called Grammie. I also wanted to be the kind of Grammie who would create the kind of love I saw in that child's eyes.

I am Grammie now. I don't know who the little spook was, but I do know there is another Grammie out there who has done something right to cause such excitement in her small grandchild's voice with the very mention of the word "Grammie."

My grandmother is the gem that
gives sparkle to my life.

Boo-Boo

Usually the first grandchild sets a precedent by naming the grandparents for all future grandchildren, but not in this case. The second-born child of our family, Kathy, was expected to call her grandmother Grandmother Shepherd, just as her older sister was already saying. But no. To this precocious child Grandmother Shepherd became Boo-Boo.

Why would a child choose Boo-Boo? Was it because her grandmother was always full of surprises, perhaps hiding and yelling "Boo," or because she could play a fun game of peekaboo? Was this child developing verbal skills around Halloween, being about ten months old at that time? The reasons seem endless.

One thing is sure though, Boo-Boo aptly fit Grandmother Shepherd, an extraordinary woman who embraced all of life, especially the surprises. And Kathy, in her ten-month-old wisdom, had pegged the perfect name for her.

My DeDaddy was dedicated to his family, delightful to be with, and dear to my heart.

—Becky Henry

DeDaddy

When my aunts and uncles began to have children, the kids called my grandfather Granddaddy or Daddy Ganus. Then my brother Dickie came along. He was just learning to talk and he would climb up in my grandfather's lap and say, "DeDaddy."

Well, my MeMaw did not like this one little bit! She kept persuading Dickie to call his grandfather Granddaddy. Soon, Dickie was saying, "GeeDeDaddy." The GeeDe" didn't sound very nice at all, so, reluctantly, my MeMaw agreed that DeDaddy would do. After some time, every one agreed it was a very cute name.

My sweet DeDaddy was the funniest man I ever knew. He would play tricks on us all the time; he loved to hear us laugh! He was also very wise. I was always impressed that he had read through every version of the Bible many times.

CT

My Children's paternal grandfather, Pop Pop, was a family practice physician. He was a rotund, jovial man—portly with gray hair. We always called him Pop Pop around the children.

When the baby of the family, at around the age of three, started calling him CT, everyone else just picked it up. We could not figure out why in the world the baby called him CT.

Finally, around Christmas, we were noticing the similarities between Pop Pop and Santa when the answer came to us. Of course! The little one was calling him Santa, and it was coming out CT. The children all called him CT for the next five years, and then he went back to Pop Pop.

How wonderful it must have been to be thought of by his grandchildren as their Santa—jolly, fat (well—maybe), and the bearer of gifts.

I love my grandfather because he always has time for me.

I'm going to ask something of every one of you. Let me start with my generation, the grandparents out there. You are our living link to the past. Tell your grandchildren the story of the struggles waged, at home and abroad, of sacrifices freely made for freedom's sake. And tell them your own story as well—because every American has a story to tell."

—George Bush

Olg

My grandmother lived through World War II. Both my father and my uncle fought in the war. For this reason, my grandmother was not real fond of the Germans at that time.

Now, my grandmother, Hilda, was a stout, rambunctious woman who did not put up with much from anyone. She had a very loud voice that carried far distances. Down deep, though she probably wouldn't want you to know it, she was a very sweet-natured woman who would do anything for you.

As a joke, because of her nature and because of her feelings about the war, my grandfather started calling her Olg. He said it was because she reminded him of the ladies over in Germany. My oldest cousin picked up on this and would tease her by calling her Old. Pretty soon, we were all calling her that. I guess she finally accepted what she couldn't change.

Now, even though I wasn't born when World War II was being fought, every time I see a documentary on television or read something in the newspaper about it, I think of Olg and of how very much I miss her.

My grandchildren come to my house once a month for dinner. My wife and I center it on some exciting event in our lives. For instance, one time we had a Civil War dinner. We cooked cornbread and beans. I dressed up in my best 1800s outfit. After dinner, we sat in our den and told stories of my great-grandfather and his family—where they were and what they were doing at the time. These are memories that my grandchildren will cherish.

A grandmother's stories build strength and
provide a foothold for integrity, dignity,
and a sense of fearlessness. They give direction,
guidance, and self-respect, define limitations,
and outline freedom.

—From *Walking in Moccasins*,
Museum of Northern Arizona,
Flagstaff, Arizona

*I love my grandmother because she is
a great storyteller.*

Young Langston Hughes curled into his grandmother's lap as she wrapped him with a bullet-riddled shawl. He stroked the tattered shawl and listened as Grandmother Langston told how her first husband Sheridan Leary, had gone to Harper's Ferry, Virginia, in 1859. She explained that Leary, a freeman, died at John Brown's side, fighting for the freedom of others, leaving the shawl behind as a symbol of his commitment to the cause.

Through Grandmother Langston's stories, Hughes learned to be courageous and to fight for his beliefs. She taught him to judge a man by his actions, not by the color of his skin, and that all people deserved to be free.

Langston Hughes died in 1967. His Kansas heritage and his grandmother's stories helped shape the words he shared with the world.

—Kansas State Historical Society

Teach your children a love of reading and you have given them a most precious gift.

∞

Remember to listen with patience.

Never turn down anything that is free.

∞

If it is to be, it is up to me.

I LOVE MY *Grandmother* BECAUSE . . .

She is very wise.

∞

She helps me say my bedtime prayers.

I LOVE MY *Grandfather* BECAUSE . . .

He brings me treats from his out-of-town trips.

∞

He takes me to the car races.

One hundred years from now it will not matter what my bank account was, the sort of house I lived in, or the kind of car I drove . . . but the world may be different because I was important in the life of a child.

I love my grandfather because he pretends to be the Beast, and I pretend to be Beauty, and we dance.

Picture your grandchildren as a rose garden. Some will bloom beautifully. Others will need to be thorned to grow. Garden with the warmth of a smile, with patience and love. In your later years, your life will be a bed of roses.

I love my grandmother because she taught me
to keep scrapbooks.

Have you ever asked yourself why your parents' mothers are called your grand-mothers? Of course you haven't because everyone with a grandmother knows that grand is the perfect word.

GranNola

When Barrett, Nola's daughter, was in the sixth grade, one of her friends laughingly told Nola, "Someday, when you are a grandmother, you will probably be called GranNola."

Years later, she did become a grandmother; and yes, her granddaughter, Hannah, calls her GranNola. It always makes for quite a laugh in the grocery store. People are so confused when Hannah calls out, "GranNola!" Does that child urgently want a granola bar? No, she wants something sweeter. She wants her grandmother, GranNola.

Mana

When I was growing up, I called my grandmother Mana. I wasn't really sure where she got the name, but it seemed to fit her so well. She was the perfect grandmother. Even though she had six grandchildren, whenever she was with you, one-on-one, she made you feel that you were the most special. She had a gift of listening without interruption to everything that was on your mind. She would respond to your questions with wisdom. She was happy, attentive, and loving. As I grew older, I wondered what the word "mana" meant. I looked it up in the dictionary. To some it was the miraculous food sent from the Lord to the Israelites on their journey to Canaan. To the Hawaiians it was a symbol of greatness: "the son." It is also defined as one with "moral authority." Now, I don't know if she was given the name because my oldest cousin couldn't pronounce "Nana" or not. But how strangely wonderful that my Mana embodies all of the definitions of the word.

Dada

I call my grandfather Dada because I couldn't say Granddaddy when I was little. I probably heard my mom and dad call him Daddy and was trying to say grand-daddy, but all I could manage was Dada.

Not many people are fortunate enough to have a grandfather who lives right down the street from them. My Dada lives that close to me, so I can go over to his house anytime I want. I enjoy being around him. He buys me many things, and he takes me many places. Sometimes we even go on vacations with him. I know I can talk to him anytime whenever I need to. He's a great listener, and all he wants in return is a smile and a hug.

He has done so much for me, and I love him a bunch. I am very thankful for my Dada!

A little boy is busily and laboriously helping his grandfather wash the car. Soon, one of his grandfather's friends comes upon the two working together on the car. "What's he paying you to help him?" the man asked the young grandson. "Attention," the boy beamed.

PePaw

My husband, Donnie, and I did not try to decide what our grandson Cody would call Donnie. We figured he would invent something, and that smart grandson of ours did not let us down.

One day when he was about two years old, I picked up Cody from day care. He loves coming to our house because we spoil him. He also loves our dog, Hootch. As soon as we got in the door, Cody ran through the house, looking for Donnie and Hootch.

"Nana, where's PePaw and Arooch?"

"What?" I asked, laughing because I had never heard these names.

"Where's PePaw and Arooch?" he asked again.

Donnie had taken Hootch for a walk. When he got home, I informed him that his new name was PePaw, and Hootch's new name was Arooch. We got the biggest kick out of this because we had never once said PaPa or Granddaddy or anything to Cody. He just came up with these names on his own. Isn't he mature and smart?

I LOVE MY *Grandfather* BECAUSE . . .

He says, "Do good and I'll help you;
do bad and I'll help you more."

∽

He says, "never lose your angel-freckles."

I LOVE MY *Grandmother* BECAUSE . . .

She helped me make my doll's clothes.
That's how I learned to sew!

❦

She gives me bubble baths.

As my grandfather always said:

If you are small, you can still be big in heart.

✧

If it's worth having, it's worth waiting for.

Pretty is as Pretty does.

∞

Be sure to say your prayers.

A grandmother recently met her friend for lunch. She started to tell her about her granddaughter and was cut short with this remark, "Before you start, I demand equal time, and I have ten grandchildren!"

If you see a book, a rocking chair, and a grandchild in the same room, don't pass up the chance to read aloud. Instill in your grandchild a love of reading. It's one of the greatest gifts that you can give.

—Barbara Bush

What is unconditional love? My first remembrance of this kind of love was with my Mamie. She was my comforter, encourager, and my biggest fan. She was a retired schoolteacher, and every night she would study with me. Once, we were conjugating Latin verbs. I was so tired of practicing that I threw a little fit and stormed from the room.

Later, feeling guilty about my behavior, I walked back to her room to apologize to her.

"David," she said, "you never need to apologize to me for anything. I know you would never do anything intentionally to hurt me."

At that moment, I knew the meaning of unconditional love. She had that for me, and I for her. Isn't that a beautiful sign of a grandmother?

"A baby is God's opinion that life should go on."

—Carl Sandburg

Honey

While vacationing in Hawaii, I found myself at the pool one day, surrounded by children playing and swimming. I kept hearing them say, "Honey, watch this!" and "Look, Honey!" At some point, I looked over to see who this Honey was that these children obviously adored. There, sitting by the pool, was their sweet, white-haired grandmother, laughing with them and clapping for their every talent.

Now that I am a grandmother, I'm teaching my grandbaby to call me Honey. I can't wait until she gets old enough to show off for me!

I love my grandmother because she says, "You are so pretty. You look just like your mommy."

Our land is everything to us . . . I will tell you
one of the things we remember on our land.
We remember that our grandfathers paid for it—
with their lives.

—John Wooden Legs, Cheyenne

Baba

My grandfather came to America from Ireland when he was fifteen years old. His father, my great-grandfather, brought his family here in search of a better future. He got a job working in a coal mine, and as soon as my grandfather was old enough, he started working there too.

I called my grandfather Baba to set him apart from my other grandfather. My Nana thinks it is a nice variation of the word *grandpa*, and I do too. After I was born, my Nana and Baba started calling me Sugar Cookie. My Nana told me that the first thing she ever cooked was sugar cookies, and they were special to her, just as I was.

My Baba died when I was just four years old. It makes me very sad to know he is gone, but I feel like he is still a very strong part of me.

Never forget those who made a difference in your life.

෫ඏ

Don't take life too seriously.

I was watching the Super Bowl with my ninety-two-year-old grandfather, and our team scored a touchdown. When they showed the instant replay, he thought they scored another one. I was going to tell him, but I figured the game he was watching was better.

—Comedian Steven Wright

I LOVE MY *Grandfather* BECAUSE . . .

He is so very funny.

∞

He let's me sleep with him when I'm scared.

He sits outside with me and we name the stars.

∞

He treats me as his friend.

∞

I feel safe when he's around.

I LOVE MY *Grandmother* BECAUSE . . .

She lets me rummage through her jewelry box.

∞

She makes great grilled cheese sandwiches.

She taught me to cook.

She gave me my mommy's doll.

She tells me funny stories about my daddy
when he was my age.

Dear Heart

My mother and I were always very close. She was at the hospital when I delivered her first grandchild. After everything was calm, she came in to spend a few minutes with me and her new granddaughter. We huddled close together and stared down at the baby. A rush of emotions flooded through her. She said that it didn't seem so long ago that she had held me just this way upon my birth.

"I want her to call me Dear Heart," she told me.

"Why, Mom?" I asked.

"Because she is the dearest thing to my heart," she replied.

She had other grandchildren after that and felt the exact same way about them. I remember her rocking them and saying, "You are just the dearest thing to my heart."

As the years passed, those children came to understand exactly what their grandmother felt—because they had that same kind of love for her.

The secret of a happy life is to skip having children and go directly to the grandchildren.

—From a MOMMA cartoon by permission of
Mel Lazarus and Creators Syndicate

Bylo

My son Larry was born during World War II. We lived in Maryland, and then moved to New Jersey. We were quite a long way from my parents, who lived in Tennessee.

After the war was over, we were finally able to make the trip down South to show off my new son! My parents were excited to meet their new grandson for the first time. My mother, Grace, would rock him and sing the song "Bylo Baby Bunting, Daddy's Gone-A-Hunting" to him. This was a very special time of bonding for my son and his grandmother.

When we got home, Larry spoke of Bylo often. Thereafter, all of her grandchildren called her Bylo. Whenever I hear this song, I fondly remember my mother holding and rocking her new grandson, and the special happiness that we all shared.

Top Ten Names for Grandmothers

1. Grandmother
2. Grandma
3. Granny
4. MawMaw
5. Nana
6. MiMi
7. Nannie
8. Me-Maw
9. Mama _____(first or last name)
10. Grandmommy

Top Ten Names for Grandfathers

1. Granddaddy

2. Grandpa

3. PaPa

4. Paw Paw

5. Granddad

6. Grandfather

7. Pop

8. Daddy _____(first or last name)

9. Paw

10. Granddaddy _____(first or last name)

Daddy Bob

I call my grandfather Daddy Bob. His real name is Robert Overton. To some, Daddy Bob might seem like a common grandfather name for anyone named Robert. It's a name I'm proud of because I am named Robert after him, and I think he is an extraordinary grandfather, very far from common.

After Daddy Bob retired, he moved to Colorado. When I was in junior high, I looked forward to visiting him on summer breaks, because he did so many cool things that boys love to do. For instance, he and a couple of other men decided to build a church in the small town where they lived. They didn't contract it out. They built it with their own hands. He put me to work on it too. When it was finished, I was proud to be able to worship in a building I had helped my grandfather and his friends build.

He was also an outdoorsman. He taught me to fish. We had great conversations, and I grew very close to him in those times. He also taught me how to camp. I remember his telling me to store the eggs and bacon away from the camp, because that's what the bears would be looking for. That really added a sense of excitement to the trip! When it snowed, he taught me how to ride a snowmobile over the Colorado land. I loved doing all of these things with him—and still enjoy them now as an adult.

One of my fondest memories is of Daddy Bob teaching me how to be a salesman. My cousin and I were visiting him one summer. He bought us a cherry orchard, and we picked cherries all day. (He paid us one dollar an hour.) When it came time to sell them, we took the "fruits" of our labor to a local Native-American reservation. I was nervous, but Daddy Bob advised me to let my customers sample the cherries. I did, and before we knew it we had sold them all!

I love him for his wisdom, his guidance, and his love of God and others. I just love him very much, and I am proud to carry his name.

Tar

My Father-in-law has always been a man with a heart for children. His years as a high school headmaster have given him much experience communicating with older children, so I imagine when he became a grandfather four times in a span of a little more than a year he was quite overwhelmed with how to deal with these smaller creatures.

He wasn't the least bit worried about what they would call him but more with how to entertain them. Consequently, my mother-in-law, BB, decided because of his cuddly demeanor and lovable personality the kids could call him Bear.

As the first four became old enough to really crawl and play he would pull down his guitar and play for the babies and sing or let them sit on his lap and pluck on the strings.

When my son started to talk he would go right in the house to my father-in-law and say "Tar!" and point to the wall where the guitar hung. Amazingly, the others, who were also on the verge of talking, followed suit and would also call for their "Tar."

Despite many efforts on the part of BB and the aunts to come up with a more suitable grandfather name, the babies refused to call their beloved grandfather anything but Tar. I think it only appropriate that a man with such a heart was given a name that really means nothing but signifies a love communicated to the heart of babies.

If you eat too much candy, your teeth will fall out.

∽

You are Grandma's precious angel!

Always be yourself, because no one will ever love you deeply if they don't know the real you.

Anything worth doing is worth doing well.

The righteous man leads a blameless life;
blessed are his children after him.

—Proverbs 20:7

Da-Daddy

On a farm in Tennessee lives J. C. Gillentine, a big, rugged man who runs a Christian camp for churches throughout the state. The camp is situated on many acres and overlooks a beautiful lake. If you visit the camp, you may see J. C. pitching hay, loading trees, or keeping up the land. But if you catch him on the right day, you might also see him playing Barbies, marbles, or horsie-ride with his three granddaughters, Caitlin (he calls her CD), Mariah (he calls her the Wind), and MacKinzie (he calls her Mac). They call him Da-Daddy, and to them Da-Daddy is a big, huggable teddy bear.

And on special occasions, you may also catch Da-Daddy on the back deck, surrounded by those three precious little girls, showing them the beauty of the lake, the wonder of nature, and the majesty of God.

Plow Jockey

My grandfather is seventy-five years old. He lives in a little town in Michigan that is made up of farmers and small shop owners. When my mom was growing up, he farmed all kinds of crops and had horses and milk cows. Since that time he has retired from farming, but he still lives in the same house in the same town with the same woman, my grandmother, who married him fifty years ago.

As a young boy, I visited my grandfather on my vacation. He would ride a plow and take me along with him. I also used to go to the shed where he stored all of the farming equipment and play on the tractors and plows. He starteed calling me a plow jockey, so I turned it around and called him one right back. Now it is our special name for each other.

My grandfather means very, very much to me, and sharing this special nickname creates a bond that I appreciate. None of my cousins have this kind of relationship with him.

Plow Jockey is a fair man. He is funny but stern when he has to be. He can always make me laugh. He appreciates every moment. He taught me to have fun and enjoy life. He has always done that. I'll always remember my grandfather as my own Plow Jockey.

You've got to do your own growing, no matter how tall your grandfather was.

—Irish Proverb

My grandmother is a great guide.
She has taught me to look forward
to new experiences and see how
bright the future is.

Grandma Sunshine

My daughter's family lives up North; my husband and I live in Florida. When my daughter and her family come to visit in the winter, my daughter always says, "We're going to see sunshine!"

Therefore, my grandchildren call me Grandma Sunshine. I take it as a great compliment because when they visit me I want them to feel warmth, happiness, and everything else that the word "sunshine" connotes.

Midwest Mammy

My mom, Kay, is affectionately referred to as Mammy by her three adoring granddaughters. Her husband, of course is called Pappy. The word "mammy" conjures up many images, but perhaps the predominant one is of a large, matronly lady from the South. But not this mammy! She is a petite, real-estate salesperson from the Midwest. Her golfing foursome cannot believe she allows herself to be called Mammy. "Kay," they insist, "you don't look or act like any mammy we have ever seen."

But Kay's first grandchild is a southern girl, born and raised in Tennessee. Kay had carefully chosen the names Grammy and Grampy for the first grandchild to call her and her husband. Nevertheless, one day "Mammy" came out of the mouth of that babe, and it sounded so endearing that it stuck.

So now, as the ladies tee off each week at the country club in Illinois, there's a mammy in the group—a very proud midwestern version.

"He thinks I'm his grandma."

"His grandma?" Harvey kept his hand on the key but didn't turn it. "You're not, are you?"

Laurie, standing behind Mattie, shook her head back and forth.

"Oh, no, but he needs one," said Mattie.

—From Walking Across Egypt by Clyde Edgerton.
© 1987 by the author. Reprinted by permission
of Algonquin Books of Chapel Hill,
a division of Workman Publishing.

*I love my grandmother because she gives me what
I need when I need it . . . and today I need ice cream.*

When I was young, my grandfather and I used to walk around his farm. I tried desperately to step exactly into his footprints. Now, twenty years later, I still try to follow those footsteps. They're just different now—they are integrity, wisdom, and love.

—Lisa Gorman

Pawp

My grandson's name is David, and he is named after me, his PawPaw. I am known for shortening the names of everyone in my family. For instance, I call my granddaughter Jessica, Jess, my daughter Gina, Gin, and my son-in-law Battle, Bat.

One day, I was sitting in my den, and David walked in, acting very big and tough for a three-year-old. "Well, hi, David!" I said as he marched through the room.

Hi, Pawp!" he said nonchalantly back to me. I loved it! He had shortened my name just like I do everyone else's.

I have six grandchildren—five who call me PawPaw and one who calls me Pawp. He is so precious to me. I guess he's a chip off the old block, not only in name, but in other ways as well.

I love my grandfather because he seems always to turn a bad situation into something good.

Do

When Dan Baccus's first grandchild, Sarah, came along, she called him DaDoo. Later her brother Stan was born, and when he was old enough to talk, he shortened the name to Do.

Do is a dentist by profession, but he is also an electrician, a plumber, and an all-around handyman. If he comes up against something he does not know how to do, he gets a book and learns how to do it. His family never has to call a repairman for anything.

One day Do had a friend visiting him. Within the course of the visit, a call came that someone had forgotten a bag of groceries at the supermarket. Do left to pick it up. Whe he returned, he fixed a car radio antenna. After that, someone dropped a contact lens down the drain, and he took the drain apart, retrieved the lens (in good shape!), and put the drain back together. His friend said to him then, "I know why they call you Do. You can *do* anything!

His friend was right! His name fits him perfectly.

Big Daddy

One of my favorite things to do is to go to the farm with my dad on Saturdays. We cut hay and play on the tractors, and sometimes we just piddle around. My grandfather, who owns the farm, is called "Big Daddy." He is as big and strong as anyone I know. He can toss more hay than my dad, even though he is older.

But Big Daddy is not only big and strong, he has a big heart. When I was a toddler, my parents lived in a house on Big Daddy's property. Not wanting to be the kind of father-in-law who would bug my mom, he kept pretty much to himself. One day my mother was on the phone with my aunt when she heard a noise outside her window.

"Ohmygosh!" she said. "Big Daddy is sitting out behind the house, revving the engine on his four-wheeler."

"What does he want?" my aunt asked my mother.

"That's his way of asking David to come out and play, but he's afraid David is napping so he won't come to the door!" My mom and aunt thought that was so

sweet! My mom took me outside, and I rode that four-wheeler all around the farm with my Big Daddy.

We no longer live on his farm, but I see him often because he's always looking for opportunities to baby-sit and teach me all about trucks, tractors, and cows. I know I will always love him in a big way—because he is my Big Daddy!

FOREIGN GRANDFATHER NAMES

Dutch: *Grootvader*

French: *Grand-père*

German: *Opa, Grossvater*

Hawaiian: *Kupuna Kāne, Tutu, Kuku*

Hungarian: *Nagyapa* Italian: *Nonno*

Italian: *Nonno*

Japanese: *Ojíisan, Sófu*

Norwegian: *Farfar, Morfar*

Polish: *Dziadek*

Portuguese: *Avô, Vovô*

Spanish: *Abuelo*

Yiddish: *Zayde*

Foreign Grandmother Names

Dutch: *Grootmoeder*

French: *Grand-mère*

German: *Oma, Grossmutter*

Hawaiian: *Kupuna wahine*

Hungarian: *Nagyanya*

Italian: *Nonna*

Japanese: *Solo, Obachan*

Norwegian *Farmor, Mormor*

Polish: *Babka*

Portuguese: *Avozinha*

Spanish: *Abuela*

Yiddish: *Bobe, Bube, Bubie*

One generation passeth away, and another generation cometh.

—Ecclesiastes 1:4

Minner

My mother's name is Mildred, and since we frequently ate lunch with her and my father, every Sunday morning on our way to church, my husband would ask me, "Are we going to Mildred's for dinner?"

When your baby is under two, you don't really think about her picking up on what you say. Of course, I had an extremely bright first child (doesn't everybody?) who was listening to our every word, and we didn't even know it.

One Sunday, when we got to my mother's to eat, my little girl looked at my mother and said, "Minner." We could not figure out why in the world she had called her grandmother Minner! We had always called her Grandmother Mildred to my daughter—and now it was Minner?

It wasn't until the next Sunday when we were in the car that my husband asked that same question: "Are we going to Mildred's for dinner?" "Bob," I said to my husband. "Mildred . . . dinner . . . Minner!" We got the biggest laugh out of the fact that our daughter had put the two together. Of course, after we explained it to my mother, she thought it was the most adorable name ever. And now, seven grandchildren later, she is Minner to the whole clan.

Honey Graham

Patsy called herself Gram when talking to her first grandchild, Cody. "This is my baby," she would say. "This is my little honey," she would coo as she cuddled the infant close to her.

When Cody was one year old, he was vacationing with Gram in Florida. As she went to pick him up, he pointed at her with great excitement and said, "My Patsy!"

No, Cody, I'm your Gram," she replied, pointing to herself.

"My Honey Graham," he announced with self-assurance and ownership.

The name said it all! A bond was sealed that day on the beach, and thereafter Patsy was called Honey Graham.

By the way, if you see a car with the license plate "Honey Graham," you'll know who is behind the wheel. The proud grandmother of Cody!

I love my grandmother because she does funny faces
to make me laugh.

Bob

I have always called my grandmother Bob. Her real name is Hettie Bob, but everybody just calls her Bob. I'm not quite sure why her parents named her a man's name. I always felt a little strange about the fact that other kids had Grandmother or Grandma—and I had Bob.

My Bob is the best! She is so funny and full of herself. I get the biggest kick out of being around her. She has the greatest stories about my mother when she was little, and I love just sitting and talking to her. Having a man's name doesn't seem to bother her in the least. It makes her unique.

But let me tell you another unusual thing about her. Hettie Bob married a man named Eddie Cobb. So they are Hettie Bob and Eddie Cobb; she is Hettie Bob Cobb. I think for now, I'll stick to calling her Bob.

G-Daddy

I call my grandfather G-Daddy. Obviously it is short for granddaddy, but another thought occurred to me. Maybe it is because he is *g*ood-looking, *g*allant, *g*racious, *g*ood-hearted, *g*entle, *g*enerous, *g*iving, and just the *g*reatest!

I love my grandfather because he tells me lots of good stories about our family.

Pop Pop

My three-year-old daughter, Leah, has a very special best buddy. She and I share a bond with this true love in her life. Her buddy is my fifty-three-year-old father whom I call Pop. Before she was one year old, Leah gave her favorite playmate and buddy the name Pop Pop. Leah is a child who is blessed with lots of love and attention from an adoring family, but her love for Pop Pop is limitless. She has his full attention and gets continuous affirmations whether she is proudly demonstrating a new ballet step or remembering two-thirds of the words from a song she has heard.

It is possible that Leah sees Pop Pop as a little person much like herself. Not only is he truly a child at heart, but Pop Pop uses a wheelchair, which makes him seem much shorter than he actually stands. Leah has such compassion for Pop Pop and understands that his legs are no longer strong enough to help him walk or run. That doesn't hamper their fun, because Leah is already learning to adapt games and adventures to accommodate a place for her buddy to roll along beside her, which is just where he wants to be! With the faith and love of a precious child, she often tells me, "When Pop Pop grows up his legs are gonna be real strong!" That's what true love is all about.

GREAT WAYS TO HELP YOUR GRANDCHILDREN REMEMBER YOU

- Build something together—a birdhouse, model airplane, or a tree house.

- Put on some music and dance together.

- Volunteer at your grandchildren's school to read, tutor, or go on field trips with them.

- Help your grandchildren start a collection you can enjoy together.

- Tell your history over and over in stories.

GREAT WAYS TO HELP YOUR GRANDCHILDREN REMEMBER YOU

- Have one-on-one time with each grandchild.

- Make buying, cutting, or decorating a Christmas tree a tradition you enjoy together.

- Tell your grandchildren about the modern conveniences available now that you didn't have growing up.

- Start a savings account for your grandchildren and add to it on special occasions.

- Take your grandchildren on a trip with you.

All of my grandparents, except one dear, sweet grandpa, were dead before I was ever born. I like to think they were the ones telling me these stories in my dreams, whispering in my ear as I was dozing off, letting me know I was loved.

—Carolyn Kay Armistead

Cupcake

My grandfather was a man of some considerable size. This, coupled with his frank manner and his booming voice, could make him quite intimidating. In my childlike innocence, however, I could see his soft and tenderhearted core. I knew he was a very loving and caring man. To me, his size was more endearing than frightening. He reminded me of a teddy bear or of Santa Claus.

Most of all, I secretly thought he looked like a giant cupcake, and that was the nickname I used for him—when he wasn't around. I'm sure as a child I may have slipped and called him that directly, but he never acted like he knew.

There was one thing I did not try to hide, though, and that was my deep affection for him. I would give anything for a big old Cupcake hug today.

Big Granny told her stories of young love and yesterdays with Granddaddy with a twinkle in her eye and her special little giggle. I feel love just remembering her.

—Deborah Andrews

BaBa

When I was a little girl, my grandmother often took me out to a farm where there were a lot of animals. There was a sheep that would always bleat at me. I am told that when the sheep would do this, I would giggle and run to my grandmother.

Whenever I wanted to go see the animals, I would look at my grandmother and say, "baa-baa." She adopted the name BaBa from me. Now, whenever I take my kids to a farm, I fondly remember the fun times in the farmyard with my BaBa.

Remember to create memories that will last forever.

∽

You know no matter what, I love you!

Hold your head high, no matter how low you feel.

∞

Happiness is success not money.

Cap

My father and many of his friends often called my grandfather, Cap, an unusual name for the man I affectionately knew as Papa. Although I never asked, I assumed that Cap was short for Captain, or maybe, I thought, it meant he was the man in charge. As I grew older, my grandfather proved to be an outstanding leader.

By the time I was ten, I had found out the origin of Cap. During the 1940s and 1950s, the mostly white residents of a small, rural Alabama community rarely discussed the plight of homeless people, much less homeless African Americans. However, Cap, a middle-aged white businessman with an eighth-grade education, did not ignore the needy. He did the unthinkable for that era. He became the guardian (official but not legal) of a young black man named Aubrey.

As if being black, homeless, and living in rural Alabama was not difficult enough, Aubrey also had epilepsy, an incurable and untreatable disease at that time. By most accounts, he would have been considered a social misfit. He felt he had nothing to live for—until he met Cap, the name he gave my grandfather the first time they met.

For more than twenty years Cap and my grandmother (Aubrey called her Old Miss) provided this poor man with the essentials for a better life: food, money, clothing, shelter, medicine, and most importantly . . . love, respect, and a feeling of self-worth.

Today, when I see a homeless person, I remember Aubrey and Cap, a most improbable pair of friends. Both now enjoy the good life in heaven. I have often wished I had asked Cap how their relationship began and what bound their friendship, but at the time it didn't seem important. I often dream about the wonderful summer days I enjoyed as a guest in the home of Cap and Old Miss and the fun times I had playing with Aubrey. Those were the times when I learned something about life and a lot about living from a loving grandfather.

Every child should be so fortunate to have a Cap!

Sugar Sweet

My grandpa's nickname is Sugar Sweet because he is so, so sweet. He loves me very much, and he acts like a kid. He is so much fun! People say when you grow up you still have a kid's personality in you. My Sugar Sweet sure does.

My mom calls my grandpa a tumble dad. He loves to spoil us. He takes us to see movies and gets us popcorn and candy. He buys us ice cream. We go to his company picnics. (He is a big businessman!) He lets us play on his computer and copy our faces on his color copier!

There is not a sweeter grandpa in the world than my Sugar Sweet. I love him soooooooo much!

Don't ever disagree with a woman.

∞

Don't be overly impressed with those in high places.
They put on their pants one leg at a time just as you do.

AS MY GRANDMOTHER ALWAYS SAID:

Tell Grandma all about it.

∽

If you see someone without a smile,
give them yours.

Maya Angelou—African-American poet whose autobiographies include many short stories told her by her grandmother.

Hans Christian Andersen—nineteenth-century Danish author whose grandmother told him folktales that he included in his stories.

Alex Haley—African-American author whose greatest success, *Roots*, was born of the genealogical history recited by his grandmother.

Langston Hughes—poet, writer, and preeminent interpreter of the African-American experience, who was raised by his grandmother.

Sir Walter Scott—often considered the inventor of the historical novel, his grandmother entertained him as a child with stories of their ancestral Scottish border country.

Eleanor Roosevelt—wife of President Franklin D. Roosevelt and activist for the poor, youth, and minorities who was raised by her grandmother.

James Madison—fourth president of the United Sates, who was tutored until age eleven by his grandmother, Frances Madison.

Sir Isaac Newton—English scientist, astronomer, and mathematician, described as "one of the greatest names in the history of human thought," who was raised by his grandmother from age three to eleven.

Alexander I—Czar of Russia (1801–25), who was taken at birth by his grandmother to supervise his preparation to assume the throne.

Hiawatha—fictional Ojibwa hero of a poem by Henry Wadsworth Longfellow, who was raised by Nokomis, his wrinkled and wise grandmother, "daughter of the Moon."

Grandmothers radiate warmth and
love. They encourage, hug,
comfort, understand,
and teach us that we are loved.

Grand Ma Ma'

My three daughters, as well as my childhood friends, have consistently teased me about being dramatic. Thus, when I joyfully learned that my eldest daughter, Brandilin, was to bear out first grandchild, I immediately began asking, "What shall I be called?"

Sorting through a series of ideas, I thought of a dramatic cutting from the play Anatasia that I performed in high school. Grand Ma Ma' seemed appropriate.

The beauty, the elation, was hearing it spoken for the first time by sixteen-month-old Virginia. Each time this now precious three-year-old says Grand Ma Ma', there is no doubt the sweetest of names was the proper one for me.

Granny Girl

She was a very young mother of an older daughter and a young nine-year-old stepdaughter. All of the "girls," as her stepdaughter would say, loved to spend time together. She would play games with them, take them to amusement parks to ride the roller coasters, and talk with them into the wee hours of the night.

When her older daughter announced that she was going to be a mother, the younger daughter protested, "You are too young to be a grandmother! I think the baby should call you Granny Girl!"

And so she was Granny Girl from then on, young at heart and full of fun.

My very favorite naming story is about Ed and Ethel, who were called the Jewish names "Zaide" and "Bubbie" by their grandson Josh.

When Josh went to nursery school, he talked continually about his Zaide and Bubbie. He told of adventures with them, and when show and tell day came, he announced that he would bring in his Bubbie and Zaide.

When he walked in with Ed and Ethel, his nursery school teacher said, "Who are these people?"

"Bubbie and Zaide," he said proudly.

"But . . . but," she stammered, "I thought they were gerbils."

—Lois Wyse, *Funny, You Don't Look Like a Grandmother*
(New York: Crown Publishing Group, 1988)

Methuselah and Noah

Methuselah was the oldest man in the Bible, and his grandson, Noah steered the ark.

William Henry Harrison and Benjamin Harrison

William was the 9th president of the United States and Benjamin was the 23rd.

Oscar Hammerstein and Oscar Hammerstein

The elder Hammerstein was a well-known German-American operatic impresario who built the Harlem Opera House and the Manhattan Opera House. The younger Hammerstein is one of the most famous American lyricists and librettists. He collaborated on some of the most memorable musicals such as *The Sound of Music* and *Oklahoma.*

Erasmus Darwin and Charles Darwin

Erasmus Darwin wrote a long poem called *The Botanic Garden,* which expounded the Linnaean system. His poem *Zoonomia* explained organic life in evolutionary terms. Charles Darwin developed the theory of organic evolution.

Tootie

As a young man, my maternal grandfather built a train in the backyard of the family home. This train later ended up at Elitch Gardens, an amusement park in Denver.

Of course, when my little brother was born, my grandfather gave him a toy train. Whenever my brother was playing with the train, my grandfather would come around the corner with another train and say, "Toot Toot! Toot Toot!" So we started calling him Tootie.

My Tootie was the kind of grandfather you could truly talk with; we would have long conversations. He and my grandmother, Mumsie, told us many family stories and created memories we will hang on to for the rest of our lives. We could see when they looked into our eyes that they were so proud of us.

My favorite recollection of Tootie was when I went to stay at their house when I was a junior in high school. I had just started dating, and my date came to pick me up at Mumsie and Tootie's house. They told me to be in by midnight. I set my grandmother's alarm clock on "slow" so that the time on the clock didn't really move every second. She didn't know I did this—or so I thought. I didn't come in until 2:00 in the morning. As I walked in the front door, I saw Tootie sitting in his chair in the living room. I was doomed!

We had a heart-to-heart chat. He told me how worried he and Mumsie had been and that if I was going to be late I should have called and that, oh, by the way, the slow speed on the clock didn't work.

I went to bed feeling terribly guilty and dreading the next day. I just knew I'd be in trouble when Mom and Dad got home. Mumsie and Tootie never told Mom and Dad about that night, at least not until many years later.

It taught me a lesson about honesty and consideration I'll never forget. "If you're running late, someone who cares about you is waiting. Call! Don't make that person worry for no reason." That was the point my grandfather wanted to make. He loved me that much. And oh, how I loved him!

Happy

Sullie is the eternal optimist. He can take a gray day and make it bright. He is joyful and always happy!

When he and his wife, Carolyn, found out they were going to be grandparents for the first time, Sullie excitedly took to the idea with great delight and began to tease Carolyn, saying, "We'll be Granny and Pappy!"

Later, enjoying every moment with his beautiful new granddaughter Leigh, he would always say, "Come to your old Pappy."

Whether Leigh couldn't say "Pappy" or whether she picked up on her grandfather's cheerful nature, when she began to talk she called him Happy.

Now, years later, Leigh and the other five grandchildren all call him Happy. Everybody's happy when Happy's around!

Children are a poor man's wealth.

—Danish Proverb

Some wise person once said that hindsight is better than foresight. That is what makes being a grandparent so wonderful! You can use all your hindsight with your grandchildren!

Bunny

When my son Jud was younger, he loved to come up to me, grab me around the waist, and compare our heights. His goal at that time was to be taller than I was (which was not that hard as I am only five feet tall—5'1" if I stretch).

And grow he did! One day, when he was in the beginning of his teens, he hugged me and realized that he had, in fact, outgrown me. "I'm bigger than you!" he said. "You feel like a little bunny!" Later, I told his brothers and sisters what Jud had said. There was an immediate, unanimous decision. "That's right! You are our little bunny and we are all going to take care of you!"

Jud kept growing—or I kept shrinking—because by the time Jud was in high school he was six feet tall, 185 lb., and a wrestler. Still, today, he will hug me up close and say "I'll take care of my little Bunny." I feel so warm and safe.

I am now the Bunny to a sweet little grandson. I look forward to the day when he comes up, grabs me, and measures himself against me to see how tall he is getting. But for now, I think this Bunny will just cuddle this little boy—and hop to do whatever he says!

Cuck

When I was very small, I discovered the cookie jar at my grandmother's house. After sneaking several cookies, my grandmother walked in and caught me. She got on to me so sternly that I started crying.

Wanting to make things right, my grandmother put her hands over her face and started opening and closing them saying "Cuckoo, cuckoo." She was trying her best to make me laugh by acting like a Cuckoo bird! Little did she know that for the next thirty years I would affectionately call her Cuck.

My grandmother had a very special recipe for rice that she handed down to me and my sisters. When she passed away, we waited a very long time before we tried to make it. Now all of us have attempted on several occasions to duplicate the recipe. It just does not taste the same! Could it be that we don't have the secret ingredient that she must have added—her special love for us? We can't be sure, but it makes perfect sense to us.

—Teresa W. Sav

I LOVE MY *Grandmother* BECAUSE . . .

She doesn't mind buying the cereal
that I see on television.

∞

She gives good hugs.

I LOVE MY *Grandfather* BECAUSE . . .

He buys tons of my school fund-raising stuff.

☙

We watch sports together.

MY GRANDFATHER

My grandfather is so big and tall
You hardly notice his wrinkles at all.
He has three corns on each of his toes
And he wears wire glasses on his nose.

He has shoes that are three sizes too big
And in his middle he looks like a pig.
He makes me laugh, he makes me giggle
When with the hoola, he does a wiggle.

He wears his overalls all the time
And sings funny songs that never rhyme.
He's a horrible cook, and I hate to say
He doesn't cook good any day.

I don't care about how he looks;
I don't care about how he cooks.
I love my grandfather, he's like no other,
And best of all he's married to my grandmother!

CowPa

Much to my paternal grandfather's chagrin, I took the name he had hoped I would call him, Grandpa, and gave it a creative twist of my own. My grandparents lived on a farm on the outskirts of a small community. Their farm had all the trappings of the Fun at the Farm books my mother read to me at night—a big red barn stacked with sweet-smelling hay, typical farm equipment, a garden filled with delicious country vegetables that would be canned for the winter, and of course, cows!

Sometimes my grandfather would lock the tractor's blade in the upright position and let me drive around the pasture, surveying the crops and stock. No one knows exactly why, but after one of our trips, I came back to the house calling him CowPa instead of Grandpa.

Neither he nor Grandma was thrilled with the nickname I had chosen. After listening to them for a little bit, I told them they were very fortunate that I had not taken my association of Grandpa and the cows one step further—to CowPaddy. They laughed and agreed—so to this day I lovingly call him CowPa.

Always pray believing.

∞

Don't ever let your children believe that you could stop loving them.

You can't be down and
out if you are up and doing.

Chew with your mouth closed.

Mu Mu

When she tried to say Mama, the baby's words came out as Mu Mu. The name stuck with this loving grandmother, who was an extraordinary woman. Mu Mu raised six children and raised them on her own. She was described by her granddaughter as "an angel on earth, a ray of sunlight when she entered the room. Someone that you loved to sit on the porch swing and talk with for hours." She was the ultimate grandmother in her grandchildren's eyes.

Bye-bye

My grandmother is hilarious. I don't remember when I was just learning to speak, but my mom has told me that my grandmother wanted to teach me to say "Bye-bye." So she would get in my face, wave, and repeat, "Bye-bye, bye-bye." It didn't matter if we had just arrived at her house, it was the middle of the visit, or we were leaving, it was time for "Bye-bye, bye-bye."

Soon this became a huge joke between my mother and my grandmother.

"What do you want her to call you?" my mother asked my grandmother one day.

"The first thing that comes out of her mouth will be my name," my grandmother responded.

With all the bye-byes that my grandmother said to me, it is no surprise that one day when I was about ten months old, I looked at her and repeated, "Bye-bye, bye-bye." "Well, I guess my name will be bye-bye," said my grandmother.

I have the fondest memories of getting to my grandmother's house and yelling "Hi-hi Bye-bye!" And of course, upon leaving, "Bye-bye, Bye-bye." I'd venture to say that I have the best Bye-bye in the world!

To-Ra

As a good Irish Catholic, Christine loved everything Irish, so she insisted that her first granddaughter be named Shannon. Shannon's mother, Christy, wanted her to call Christine Monny-Mom, which she had called her grandmother. Monny-Mom was apparently a variation of Mommy's Mom, and Christy always talked to Shannon about Christine as Monny-Mom.

From the time Shannon came home from the hospital, Christine would sit and rock her and sing "too-ra-loo-ra-loo-ral" to her. It is the Irish lullaby that has the singer remembering her mother singing it many years ago and willing to "give the world if she could sing that song to me today."

Shannon's first word to her grandmother, when she was nine months old and walking in the door to visit, was To-Ra. She called her To-Ra ever after, as did other grandchildren and great-grandchildren. Even Christine's husband and children often referred to her as To-Ra, and the engraving on her tombstone includes that name—To-Ra.

Over in Killarney
Many years ago
Me mother sang a song to me
In words so soft and low

A simple little ditty, in her
sweet old fashioned way
I would give the world to hear
her sing this song today.

Too-ra-loo-ra-loo-ral
Too-ra-loo-ra-li
Too-ra-loo-ra-loo-ral
Hush now don't you cry.

Too-ra-loo-ra-loo-ral
Too-ra-loo-ra-li
Too-ra-loo-ra-loo-ral
That's an Irish lullaby.

I LOVE MY *Grandfather* BECAUSE . . .

He picks me up after school and takes me to get an Icee!

∽

He showed me how to bait my hook and catch big fish.

I LOVE MY *Grandmother* BECAUSE . . .

She taught me to tie my shoelaces.

∞

When I think of her, I can smell her spaghetti sauce.
It is the best and so is she!

I love my grandmother because when I was three years old, she was telling me a very long story, and I asked her to please let her mouth go night-night. She didn't get mad, and she laughs about it to this day.

Boo-Boo Nana

His earliest recollection of his grandmother was with a broken arm. In fact, it seemed to him that his grandmother always had some sort of boo-boo. Both he and his grandmother found it extremely funny that every time he saw her she had had another sort of accident. When his parents would say they were going to Nana's, he would call out, "Are we going to Boo-Boo Nana's?" This was how he could distinguish the two grandmothers in his life.

She dearly took to the name of Boo-Boo Nana and not accidentally, she is called that to this day by all of her grandchildren.

My grandma is in heaven, but when I do something special, my mom says, "I'm so proud of you, and Grandma would be, too."

If youth but had the knowledge
and old age the strength.

—French Proverb

I love my grandfather because he gave me my first Bible with a very special note in it from him to me.

Pow Pow

My mother had one rule when I was little: "He will not own a toy gun. There will be no play shooting, no army men!" she announced. Well, to my grandfather, that was like saying I had to wear dresses! All little boys play with guns, he argued, whether the game was cowboys and Indians, army, or whatever!

So when he would baby-sit me, it was our little secret. We would play everything that you could imagine using our thumb and pointer fingers as pretend guns. I would sneak around the corner and shoot him, saying, "Pow! Pow!"

"Ugh! You got me!" he would say, grabbing his chest and falling to the floor. From that secret play I began to call him Pow Pow. My mom always thought it was another version of Paw Paw, but my grandfather and I knew different. It was a name that brought a smile to his face then—and still does now.

Ikey Pop

I call my grandfather Ikey Pop. His real name is Isodore Price Keller, but his nickname has always been Ikey. When I was little, all I ever heard him called was Ikey, so I assumed that was his one-and-only name. I refused to call him Grandpa. When my mother tried to correct me, I wouldn't listen to her.

She tried to get me to call him Grand Pop—which I turned into Ikey Pop. After much frustration on my mother's part, she finally just gave in. I was the first grandchild, so he is now called Ikey Pop by all of the grandchildren. I think it is a wonderful name. I think he is a wonderful granddaddy!

I LOVE MY *Grandfather* BECAUSE . . .

He takes me fishing.

&

He is kind and always takes up for me.

I LOVE MY *Grandmother* BECAUSE . . .

She taught me to knit.

∞

She's my sweetie pie, and I'm her sweetie pie.

Grandmothers don't have to do anything but be there.

Around the Corner Nano

My grandmother lived, guess where? Around the corner. When my mother would go over to her house, she would yell to my dad, "I'm going around the corner!" "Where's Momma?" I would ask. "She's at Nano's, around the corner," he would answer.

Soon, we all just referred to her as Around the Corner Nano. "Around the Corner Nano is having dinner for us tonight", "Did you hear what Around the Corner Nano said today?" I've always been grateful for the fact that my grandmother and I were very close—just around the corner, in fact.

Mopsy

My daughter and I are blessed with blonde hair. Lots of blonde hair. Lots of curly, blonde hair. In fact, I am proud of the fact that there is no mistaking that Angela is my daughter. She looks just like me!

Of course, with the kind of hair that we have, we sometimes have difficulty getting it to look like we want it to. Not long after my first grandbaby was born, Angela was visiting. I was in the bathroom ranting and raving that I couldn't do anything with this mop of hair that I had. She teasingly called me Mopsy. Then she began to call my husband Popsy.

Guess what my grandbaby calls me now? And you know what? I love it! I figure that it's much better than Flopsy or Cottontail!

If your baby is beautiful and perfect, never cries or fusses, sleeps on schedule, and burps on demand, an angel all the time . . . you're the grandma.

—Teresa Bloomingdale

Carrots make your eyes strong.

Come let me kiss it.

Stay away from fire ants.

You can never love someone you haven't laughed with.

You didn't think it's possible to love your grand-children any more than you do today . . . but then tomorrow comes.

—Author Unknown

MD

My father is a Ph.D. and a lovable eccentric. When my husband and I were dating, he would come to my house to pick me up and find my father on our roof. Dad was reroofing at the time. Dad would yell down a greeting to my husband and actually carry on a conversation with him from the roof.

My husband was so amused by this white-bearded professor and their rooftop chats that he immediately began calling him the Mad Doctor to all of his friends. The name eventually leaked out, and luckily, my father was a good sport about it. I mean, he did let me marry the guy. Over the years Mad Doctor was shortened to MD. Sixteen years later, my children, Lee, age nine, and Dawson, age five, love calling him MD and get a bigger kick out of hearing the story.

I LOVE MY *Grandfather* BECAUSE . . .

He believes in me.
He always says, "You can do it! Just try!"

∞

He rides me on his lawn mower.

I love my *Grandmother* because . . .

∞

She tells me I am perfect.

∞

She taught me how to plant a garden.

In relating the blessings that have come their way, grandmothers teach us gratitude.

Ma'am

I wanted to be called Gram by my grandchildren. I also wanted my grandchildren to have nice manners. For this reason, I think I thoroughly confused their little minds.

When I would call them and they would say, "Huh?" or "What?" I would say, "Ma'am" or "Yes, ma'am."

"Do you want a sandwich?"

"No."

"No what?"

"No ma'am."

"Good."

Pretty soon, my granddaughter would run into my kitchen and say, "Ma'am milk." So now Gram has changed to Ma'am and I am the well-mannered grandmother. Thank you very much!

Go-Go

When I was younger, I used to hear all of the kids at school talking about their grandmothers. "Grandmother got me this." "Grandmother said that." I didn't understand why I didn't have a grandmother.

Finally, one day, I went home very sad.

"What's wrong?" my mother asked me.

"Everybody has a grandmother except me," I choked out to my mother, trying to hold back the tears.

"Why, Marsha," my mom said. "Everybody has a grandmother, but not everybody has a Go-Go. You have a Go-Go!"

I had always called my grandmother Go-Go. My older cousin had given her that name. I didn't know she was my grandmother! I just knew that whenever I visited her home, we would go all kinds of different places, like to the store, or the park, or the library. She lived in California, and before we even got our bags unpacked, she would excitedly begin to tell us about all the things we were going to do and the places she had planned to go. I was always excited to go to Go-Go's house because I knew that she would have somewhere interesting and new to take me.

As I grew older and the kids talked about their grandmothers, instead of feeling left out and sad, I straightened my shoulders and thought to myself, "They may have a grandmother, but I have a Go-Go!" I was very proud.

I love my grandmother because she puts my art all over her refrigerator.

I LOVE MY *Grandmother* BECAUSE . . .

We sit outside at night and talk about anything
I want to talk about.

∽

She is a good listener.

I LOVE MY *Grandfather* BECAUSE . . .

He taught me to use a tire gauge and to change a tire.

∞

He puts me on his shoulders at the Christmas parade.

Give a little love to a child and
you get a great deal back.

—John Ruskin

Granddaddy Bro

Mr. William is a concierge at a hotel in Knoxville, Tennessee. He is the father of five, the grandfather of four, and the great-grandfather of one.

He has always been the type to lend a hand or an ear to anyone in need of help. He worked at a hospital for thirty years, drives the church van, takes care of his invalid wife, and now works at the hotel. He always, always has a smile.

When he was growing up, everyone called him Bro. It was an endearing term, an expression of affection. When his first son was born, the boy picked up on the name and called him Bro instead of Daddy. All of the children followed that lead. So, of course, when his grandchildren were born, they called him Granddaddy Bro.

Granddaddy Bro wakes up every day and thanks God for the wonderful life he has. It is certain that his family does the same—except we're sure that each day they also thank God for a wonderful man like Granddaddy Bro.

King

My father has always called me his little princess. He is a very sweet and kind man who loves to give big hugs. I remember many times when he would come home from work and sit in his big lounge chair. I would sit in his lap, and he would say, "How was your day, Princess?" I always knew I was very special to him.

The years passed so fast. It wasn't long until I was married and had a very active little girl of my own. My father was so delighted when my daughter was born. He calls her his "little angel." He was very careful not to call her Princess—after all, that title belonged to me!

My daughter called him Granddaddy up until the time she was six years old. I'll never forget the night when we were at my parents' house for dinner. Daddy was sitting in his lounge chair and my daughter was sitting on the floor playing. As I walked into the room he motioned for me to sit in his lap. I sat down and hugged his neck. "How are you doing, Princess?" he asked. My daughter had heard him call me this before, but she had never said anything. It was as if she had heard it for the first time. She stopped playing and looked at my father.

"Granddaddy, why do you call my mommy Princess?" she asked.

"Because she's my little princess," he answered. "Do you know that no matter how old your mommy gets she will always be my princess?"

"Well," said my very astute six-year-old, "if she is your princess that must mean that you are a king and Grandmommy is the queen!"

We laughed at that. "I guess you're right," he said. That is the night we started calling Granddaddy and Grandmommy King and Queen.

One night as my father and I were standing in the kitchen watching my daughter and her new baby brother playing together, he put his arm around me, leaned over, and whispered, "I may not be as monetarily rich as a king, but oh, look at the riches I have." I hugged him so tight! He is definitely royalty in all of our sights.

I LOVE MY *Grandfather* BECAUSE . . .

He treats me like a princess.

∞

He tells me I'm pretty.

I LOVE MY *Grandmother* BECAUSE . . .

She fixed a special room at her house for me!

∽

She taught me about God. I always sat by her at church.

Timothy learned about God from his mother and grandmother when he was a small boy.

—II Timothy 1:5

One time I went to Grandma's house, and we made about thirty cookies in all different shapes. I took some home to my brothers, and now every time I go to Grandma's house we always make a lot of cookies.

—Brett Henry

Trixie

Her children and grandchildren called her Trixie. Our friends lovingly referred to her as Miss Trixie. My grandmother had a warm smile, a hearty laugh, and a quick wit. But it was her tricks for making every task easier that got her the name of Trixie. Whether playing a game, learning to bake, or memorizing Bible verses, my grandmother could find a shortcut. We referred to this as "Trixie's little bag of tricks." She used her love for cooking to make people feel special. Her friends and her children's friends were the recipients of her yummy cakes and rolls. I remember trying to make a cake with her one day. Watching her mix the batter would leave me wondering how they could taste so good. You soon realized that she had her own little bag of tricks, such as a "dash" of this or a "pinch" of that. I find myself using many of her tricks in my day-to-day life now. And whenever I do, her knowing smile enters my mind and brings joy to my heart.

Mama Too

The oldest of five children, I was first to marry and first to present my parents with a grandchild. We lived close to my parents and visited often. We all called my mother "Mama." I had a little brother just eight years old when my baby, Virginia, was born.

Whenever we would visit, Virginia would hear me, my three sisters, and her eight-year-old uncle call my mother Mama. One day, in her wide-eyed innocence, she went up to my mother and asked, "Are you my mama, too?"

"Yes I am!" she said. And from that moment on, she has been Mama Too to all ten of her grandchildren.

Becoming a grandmother is like having dessert. The best is saved for last.

GRANDMOTHERS ARE TO LOVE

For the most valued jewel of Grandma's
Is not a diamond or topaz,
But the precious little child
That her child now has.
You've a very special trust.
Remember this . . . please do.
The love of generations
Is handed down to you.
So if you have a grandma
Thank the good Lord up above,
And give Grandmama hugs and kisses,
For grandmothers are to love.

  —Lois Wyse, *Funny, You Don't Look Like a Grandmother*
    (New York: Crown Publishing Group, 1988)

I love my grandmother because she has shown me how to pause, enjoy the moment, and see the beauty that surrounds me.

Boddy

The Tennessee State Fair of 1945 was held in my hometown. Back then it was not customary for schools to let students out of class to attend such events without a note from the parents. A creative set of twins, Billy and Bobby, along with a neighborhood friend, were not going to let their lack of a note from their parents stand in the way of a day filled with rides, shows, and cotton candy. They conjured up a very creative plan—they thought. The friend wrote a note that said, "Please let Billy and Boddy (instead of Bobby) out of school to go to the fair. Thank you, Mrs. Beulah Teal."

The boys failed to proofread the note before they turned it in to their teacher. Needless to say, the teacher caught the misspelling, and they did not get to attend the fair that day. From then on, Billy used the nickname Boddy for his twin brother.

Years passed, and Bobby's grandchildren were coming along. He did not want to be called Grandfather of Granddaddy. During this time of decision, he related the state fair story to us. We chose Grandboddy as his grandfather name, which the grandchildren have now shortened to just Boddy.

I LOVE MY *Grandfather* BECAUSE . . .

He gives great hugs and sweet sugar kisses.

∞

He plays the guitar for me.

He sings silly songs in a silly voice and makes me laugh.

∞

He loves me unconditionally.

∞

He answers all my questions; he knows
almost everything.

I LOVE MY *Grandmother* BECAUSE . . .

She comes to all of my ball games.
Afterward, she takes me to the concession stand
and lets me buy whatever I want.

∞

She made me a quilt.

She always let me drink out of her fine china cups when I was a child. I am seventy years old, and I still drink my coffee from a fine china cup.

∞

She loves me no matter what.

∞

My secrets are safe with her.

In the end it's not the years in your life that count, it's the life in your years.

—Abraham Lincoln

Uncle Daddy

For years, we didn't know that Uncle Daddy was not what all grandchildren called their grandfathers. Believe it or not, my grandmother had her last child one day after her oldest child, Aunt Dot, had her first baby! My Uncle Pat was one day younger than his nephew Tommy!

When Aunt Dot brought little Tommy to meet the family, my Uncle Johnny was introducing the baby around. He said, "This is your Uncle Phil, this is your Uncle Mike, this is your Uncle Pat" (a baby himself!) When he got to my grandfather he said, "And this is your Uncle Daddy!"

All of us grandchildren who came along afterward adopted the name and called our grandfather Uncle Daddy. Of course, our grandmother was Aunt Momma. These names made them feel young—and they really were! They had just had a baby themselves!

SWEET GRANDPA

How sweet the sound of Grandpa
When he calls my name to come . . .
As he tells me over and over
That I'm his lovely one.

How sweet the smell of Grandpa
When he comes in from the wind . . .
When he cooks my favorite breakfast
And he treats me like a friend.

How sweet the sight of Grandpa
When I'm acting in my play
Or at the front door of his house
When I go to stay.

How sweet the feel of Grandpa
When he hugs me up real close
Or as he carries me to my bed . . .
These times I treasure most.

My grandpa is felt in my senses
When we're together or when we're apart.
My grandpa is felt deep inside of me,
Way down . . . in the depth of my heart.

—Mindy Henderson

Great Ways to Help Your Grandchildren Remember You

- Make a tape recording of special memories of your family history, of their parents' experiences, or of your feelings the first time you held them.

- Find out what their favorite food is and always have that available to them whenever they are at your house.

- Sing a special song to them each time they are around.

- Share your spiritual beliefs with them.

Great Ways to Help Your Grandchildren Remember You

- Develop a special code—whether it be a look, a pat, or a phrase that is special between only the two of you.

- Start a tradition with them that is special only to them. For instance, send them a special flower on their birthday every year.

- Read to them.

- Give your grandchildren something that is special to you, and it will always remind them of you.

I don't know who my grandfather was; I'm much more concerned to know who his grandson will be.

—Abraham Lincoln

Teach by example, not words.

∞

If it sounds too good to be true, it probably is.

PaPa

When we learned our first grandchild was on the way, Linn, my wife, named herself Gran. That was settled. Gran was the perfect name for her; it suited her to a *T*.

But what about me? What fit me best? What sounded right to go along with Gran?

For months we tried to settle on a perfect grandfather name. Eventually, we came up with Granddad. It sounded good with Gran-Gran and Granddad. But we weren't convinced it was right.

Finally the big day arrived. Our daughter Becky was in labor. Aubrey Sara was on the way! As we stayed in the waiting room with our son-in-law, Phil, pacing the floor and praying for a safe delivery, all of a sudden a lightbulb turned on inside of my head. It was June 21—my own deceased grandfather's birthday. He was a fine and stately gentleman—a college president revered by everyone—and all his children and grandchildren had called him PaPa.

"That's it," I said. "Aubrey is being born on PaPa's birthday. I shall be called PaPa!"

And so we became PaPa 'n' Gran. I love to hear Aubrey and Davis call me PaPa.

It links me to my past and brings back such fond memories. However, I admit that once in a while when they call me Pops or Poppy as a term of endearment, that's when I truly melt.

GRANDMOTHERS ARE TO LOVE

I reached out for the hands to hold
To guide me through the mall
My grandma took good care of me
When I was very small

And as I grew she saw in me
The things I didn't know
She always said you're good inside
Your heart will grow and grow . . .

I reached out for the hand to hold
That made my clothes for me
That cooked my favorite cookies
And bandaged my knee.

That wiped tears from my eyes . . .
Picked flowers for my hair . . .
And intertwined each time
That we would say a prayer.

I reached out for the hands to hold
Before I went down the aisle
To marry the man I loved with
The approval of her smile.

And as grandma got older
I'd consult her for advice
She'd patiently sit and talk with me
Oh . . . our talks were so, so nice.

Now the years have come and gone
Though it's hard to understand.
Now when I am with her . . .
She reaches for my hand.

I gladly take good care of her
I hold her in my heart . . .
And as I hold her hand I know
We'll never be apart.

—Minday Henderson

I love my grandmother because she says that there is no one like me! I am a masterpiece! I am special!

I LOVE MY *Grandmother* BECAUSE . . .

She lets me brush her hair and play beauty shop.

∞

She spoils me rotten.

I LOVE MY *Grandfather* BECAUSE . . .

He gave me my great-grandfather's pocket watch.

∞

He helps me with my homework.

My grandfather once told me that there are two kinds of people: those who work and those who take the credit. He told me to be in the first group; there was less competition there.

—Indira Gandhi

Ogre

When I was in high school I was an average teenager, but my father was very strict. When it came to curfews, friends, boyfriends, school, whatever, he always made it very clear to me that it was "his way or the highway."

One night when I had missed my curfew, he was waiting at the door for me. We got into a huge fight, and finally I yelled out, "You are just a big ogre!" Well, guess what. That name stuck!

Now that he is a grandfather and has matured and aged—he has not changed a bit! He is still set in his ways and very stubborn, and when someone makes him mad I'm pretty sure his eyes glow red—just like an ogre!

All of his grandchildren call him Ogre. He loves us all very much and we all love him, and he thinks the name Ogre is funny. We still think he carries all of the characteristics associated with the name. I guess he's a lovable Ogre—if there is such a thing!

Big Buddy

From the minute I first laid eyes on my grandson, he and I have had a very strong bond; I've always called him my little buddy. One day we were spending our special time together, and I called him Little Buddy. He looked up and smiled at me and called me Big Buddy. He had figured that out all by himself! I was so proud of my smart grandson!

He is now nine and has a brother who is five. We go on hikes and fishing trips, go to ball games, and spend as much time together as we can. We are all best friends—and best buddies.

*I love my grandfather because he lathers me up
and lets me "play shave" with him.*

Grossmutter Grossie

When I was a little girl, my family took a trip from San Diego to Indiana every summer to visit my mother's family. The thing I remember most was visiting with my great-grandmother, Grossie. She was my mother's grandmother, and she helped raise my mom and her sister and brother. I remember distinctly arriving at Grossie's house and seeing this little old woman with hair as white as cotton (and just as soft) come out to greet us. She was always so interested in everything that we had to say! She would ask us questions about what interested us. We would try to rush through her questions however, because our favorite part of visiting Grossie was hearing all of her stories about when she was a young girl.

Grossie is short for Grossmutter, German for "grandmother." Grossie moved to the United States when she was very young. My favorite story concerns one of her very first jobs in the States, as a nanny at the age of fifteen. One day while she was out with her charges, a horse and carriage careened through the street and was going to hit Grossie and the children. She pushed the kids to safety and was trampled by the carriage. She was rushed to the doctor who told her mother that she would probably not live, and if she did, she wouldn't be able to have children. When she would tell me this story, it became so real I could see the horse and carriage coming and my Grossie saving the little ones. I would get the warmest feeling inside. The amazing thing about this story is that she not only lived to be ninety-five years old, but she was also the mother of two very healthy children.

In America, the word "gross" describes things that are less than appealing. To me, my Grossie was the sweetest living angel that God ever put on earth.

I love my grandmother because we sit outside at night, look at the sky, and talk about anything I want to talk about.

A little boy had bought his grandmother a book and wanted to inscribe the front with something really special. He racked his brain and suddenly remembered that his father had a book with an inscription that he was very proud of. So the little boy decided to copy it. You can imagine his grandmother's surprise when she opened her book, which was the Bible, and found it inscribed, "To Grandma, with the compliments of the author."

I love my grandmother because when my dad gets after me, she reminds him that I am just like him.

I love my grandfather because he prays with me.

A grandfather was walking through his yard when he heard his granddaughter repeating the alphabet in a tone of voice that sounded like a prayer. He asked her what she was doing. The little girl explained, "I'm praying, but I can't think of exactly the right words, so I'm just saying all the letters. God will put them together for me, because he knows what I am thinking."

Hot Dog

Of all their seven grandchildren, my nephew Tyler was the one my parents spent the least amount of time with. When he spent a week with them one summer he had not decided what to call them. (They're Nana and Granddaddy to all of the other grandchildren.)

So Mom and Daddy were suggesting all the old standards like Granddad, Pop Pop, Paw Paw, and Tyler kept saying a strong "no" to everything they brought up. Finally, I guess my mother was a little weary of going through all the names, and as she got tired, she got a little silly. When she offered Hot Dog to Tyler as a name for my dad, he lit right up and said, "That's it!" Now, my dad is the most humble, soft-spoken, sweet man you would ever meet. He is not at all the show-off that the name Hot Dog connotes, but to Tyler he is a very special Hot Dog indeed.

If you show respect, you will get respect.

You're not fully dressed until you're wearing a smile.

When you're pointing a finger at someone, there are always three pointing back at you.

∞

If you don't know where you're going, you probably won't get there.

Boo-Daddy

When my sorority sisters were conducting a late-night discussion on what we called our grandparents, there was no question that Laney's grandfather took the cake for having the most amusing nickname.

When his first grandchild was little, Laney's grandfather loved to sneak up on her and teasingly startle her with a resonating, "BOO!" They played this game all the time, and without fail, his antics sent the child into peals of laughter. Soon, everyone in the house was laughing too.

Laney said her grandfather is very sweet and full of surprises. It did not take long for his grandchildren to begin calling him Boo-Daddy. He's living up to that nickname today for his great-grandchildren too.

*A good grandmother keeps
the vision of beauty and instills
the hope in her children and
grandchildren.*

Big Mama

When my first grandchild was just walking, he came into my house crying because he had fallen and gotten a "boo-boo."

"Come see Big Mama," I said to him. I picked that small, sweet child up in my arms. I kissed his hurt and dried those tears. I carried him back to my big rocking chair that had been handed down to me from my grandmother. He curled up in my lap. I sang to him and rocked him to sleep. I bet we rocked together, my grandson and I, for at least an hour.

To some, Big Mama would be an insult. But, to my small grandson, I am big. And to him, big means secure. So I am not insulted. Because there is nothing in the world finer than my grandchild cuddling in the security of my arms in that rocking chair.

Moms

My grandmother, Moms, was a woman ahead of her time. She had lost her own mother to cancer when she was just five years old, so she grew up to be very independent. After my father was born, she was divorced and had to work to support my dad and herself. She continued to work even after she remarried, which was unusual for a woman in the 1950s.

When she became a grandmother, she felt she was still too young to be called Granny, so she chose the name Moms for herself. My childhood memories of Moms include going to movies, visiting her office, and eating the most fantastic Christmas Eve dinner every year, consisting of all of my favorite foods.

I always believed that Moms was a special person, but I realized what a true fan I had when I decided one summer to move three thousand miles away to see if things would work out with the man I loved. All of my friends and other family members thought I was crazy. Moms, on the other hand, told me a story about how she packed everything that she owned into a car and moved two hundred miles away to

marry her second husband and true love. I went with her blessing and support. Now I'm married to this wonderful man and we have two precious children. My family and I have since returned and now live less than a mile from this very special eighty-four-year-old grandmother and now great-grandmother, Moms.

LOVE MY *Grandmother* BECAUSE . . .

She likes to have tea parties with me.

∞

She has pictures of me all over the house.

She is the best biscuit maker in the world.

She takes me on fun trips to places like Disney World.

She makes every holiday and birthday
a very special occasion.

I LOVE MY *Grandfather* BECAUSE . . .

He calls me a special nickname.

∞

He taught me to play golf—and even
made me my first clubs!

He taught me to read a map.

⚭

He gave me my first cowboy hat.

⚭

He treats all my friends to burgers after our ball games.

Treat the earth well; it was not given to you by your parents, it was loaned to you by your children. We do not inherit the Earth from our ancestors, we borrow it from our children.

— Native-American Proverb

Daddy Green

Every little boy and girl would consider it a dream come true to have a grand-daddy with a candy store. For my siblings and me that dream did come true. Our Daddy Green owned a grocery store in Leiper's Fork, Tennessee. The moment we stepped into the store to visit, we would go behind the big counter and get our own big brown paper bag. These bags would then be filled with candy, gum, peanuts, Crackerjacks, and anything else we wanted!

Daddy Green had a special love for all children. A child never left his store without at least a lollipop given to them by our grandfather. Now Green's Grocery is on the Historical Register and has become famous. It gives me such pride to know that that was my grandfather's store. I have wonderful, fond memories of that big, old candy showcase and of my sweet grandfather—whose sweetness surpassed all of the candy in the world.

Kookyfoo

The name Kookyfoo came about in the games that Bob Whitaker played with his grandchildren, in which an imaginary language was spoken to describe people and events—much akin to the phonetic, but artificial language entertainer Sid Caesar used in his television skits.

Young children have vivid imaginations that lead to exciting adventures if you enter into their world at their level. Kookyfoo did just that, unlocking the door to that world where the only limit is the extent of one's own imagination and where a special language becomes the vehicle to travel to the farthest frontiers. Porch swings were transformed into space vehicles to take everyone to the edge of the solar system, where "Pluto wagged its tail," "a sea monster swam and reared its head on Neptune," and the "Milky Way was an ice cream shop."

As the grandchildren (ages seven through fourteen) accompanied their grandfather on one of these imaginary adventures, the conversation between them and Granddad took on the form of "crazy talk"—languages that could sound like a mix-

ture of Chinese, Russian, German, etc. Kookyfoo came out as a name for a particular grandchild traveling the stars with Granddad at that moment. The others were so tickled over the name that they began turning it back on their grandfather!

"Who's Kookyfoo?" Granddad Bob would say when greeting one of the children. They quickly learned to respond, "You are!"

The mental image of a loving grandfather may be a piece of the picture that his grandchildren carry to maturity as a part of their concept of godliness. What an opportunity! What a gift! What a responsibility! Oh, that I can make a difference, an eternal difference, in the lives of children.

—David Booth

I love my grandfather because when I was young, he took me on long walks. We would rest under a tree, and he would say, "Take time to look around you and see the beauty."

I love my grandmother because she is pretty and so sweet. She loves me and all of my cousins equally. She says we are like the flowers in her garden. Each of us has a unique beauty.

Grandmothers don't have to be smart. They just have to know how to answer questions like, "Is God married?" and "Why do dogs chase cats?"

I love my grandmother because when she sees me,
just the look on her face says, I love you.

Boat Grandma

When my brother and I were young, our father's business transferred him all over the world. Visits with our grandmothers were a rare treat, requiring travel over a long distance and a stay of several nights.

You know how it is when you sleep in a different house, in a different bed. You hear every little noise, every creak and pop. One of our grandmothers lived on an island on the St. Clair River in Michigan. At night, the huge lake and ocean freighters would signal, especially in the fog. It didn't take two young boys long to recognize those special night sounds as comforting noises that made us feel safe because we were at Boat Grandma's house.

We are now twenty-two and twenty-eight years old. Whenever we hear those special night sounds, they rekindle warm memories of our youthful visits to our Boat Grandma—who just turned eighty-nine!

Bink

When my first granddaughter was born, my daughter Debbie decided that she should call me by my first name, Sue. Sara, my granddaughter, had a hard time saying her S's. One day I stopped by to visit them on my lunch hour from work. As I was about to leave, Debbie said, "Sara, tell Sue good-bye!" Sara didn't respond.

"Sara, tell Sue good-bye," Debbie said once again. "She has to go back to work at the bank."

Sara still did not respond. But as I neared the bottom of the steps to leave, she ran up behind me and said, "Bye-bye, Bink."

You know, I handle money every day at the bank. And to some people that is where they store their treasures. But not for me. Mine is in the three adorable grandchildren who call me Bink.

We're called Lolly and Pop by our grandchildren. Are we suckers for them? You bet we are!

—Lanell Padgett

I LOVE MY *Grandmother* BECAUSE . . .

She comes to my piano recitals.

∽

When I spend the night at her house, I am always
awakened by the smell of bacon, and I know that a big
breakfast is waiting for me!

She hired a clown to come to my birthday party!

∞

If my mommy is working, she comes and picks me up at school and takes care of me when I am sick.

∞

She puts my juice in a coffee mug so I can feel big.

I LOVE MY *Grandfather* BECAUSE . . .

He showed me how to whittle sticks so that I could
cook hot dogs over a fire.

❧

He helps me with my paper route.

He gives me great business advice and makes me see things from different perspectives.

He teases my grandmother and hugs on her.

He didn't graduate from college, but he knows secrets to growing crops. He can also read people better than any college graduate I know.

My grandfather is sacred to me.
Sometimes when I close my eyes,
I can feel his spirit move through
me like the wind. It reminds me
that he lives on through me
and my children.

Not a tenth of us who are in business are doing as well as we could if we merely followed the principles that were known to our grandfathers.

—William Feather

Popeye

My father is a very strong man. When I first took my children to visit him they were amazed at his big, muscular arms. He would pull his sleeve up and let them touch his muscle. They couldn't believe it! After watching him eat a big salad one night, my son Alexander looked up at me. "Was that spinach he just ate, Daddy? He's just like Popeye!"

It is so funny what kids can put together. Of course Popeye became his name right then.

Now my kids eat lettuce to get strong like Popeye. (I can't bring myself to tell them that it's not spinach, although sooner or later they will figure it out.) And whenever my kids see the cartoon or hear the song "I'm Popeye the Sailor Man," they immediately think of their very own big, strong Popeye.

God gave you two eyes, two ears,
and one mouth, so you should watch and
listen twice as much as you talk.

Pa

Everyone in the small town where my grandparents lived called them Ma and Pa. My Pa was an endearing man, and everyone loved him, but I loved him the most.

Whenever I got to choose a baby-sitter, I would choose Pa. Even though I was terrified of bugs and snakes as a small girl, I loved going with him into the garden on his farm to pick watermelons in the summer and pumpkins in the fall.

He didn't have a lot of money, but he was always looking for reasons to give me a dollar. He would give me money for good report cards. He even gave me a dollar every time I got my hair cut!

The thing I remember most about him, however, is that he treated his six children, fourteen grandchildren, and twenty-four great-grandchildren equally. He had abundant love for his family, and he heaped it upon us until the day he died. I still miss him to this day.

Paddycake

When my oldest child, Brian, was a baby, we only saw my parents every few months or so. But whenever we visited, my dad would always put Brian on his lap and play patty-cake with him. It made Brian laugh until he was nearly out of breath. Brian came to expect the patty-cake game with my dad, and he started calling him Granddaddy Patty-cake (now shortened to just Paddycake). He did this to distinguish his two granddaddies.

The name seemed appropriate also because my dad loves to bake, and he sometimes lets Brian help him in the kitchen, now that he is older. Other grandchildren have come along, and they also call this granddad their Paddycake.

My brother recently married. His new wife, wanting to be in on the family lingo, addressed my dad by his nickname. Unfortunately, she didn't remember it quite right and called him Popcorn! We all found it amusing. Now my dad may end up going by either name—which is fine with him.

Grandparents and grandchildren have much to tell each other. One has just come from the spirit world and the other is on his way to the spirit world.

—Tautachcho, Chumash people

I can still picture my grandmother, pulling her rocking chair beside the table on which her old rotary phone sat. She would take her shoes off and put her feet on the air vent, which was right below the table. I can see her performing this ritual every day—calling to check on our grades, to find out how our day went, and to tell us that she loved us.

Ha-Ha

My mother had four children of her own, but the prospect of becoming a grandmother left her somewhat anxious. Whenever my mother was with her first grandchild, she would get right in her face and pretend to laugh: "ha-ha-ha!" She would get the result that she was looking for when my precious little daughter would look at her and smile. This happened at each and every visit. "Ha-ha-ha!"

When my daughter Brenda was nearing two years old, my mother came once again to visit. As she walked through the door, Brenda ran to her and screamed, "Ha-ha!" Laughing, my mother picked her up and the name just stuck. Everyone in the family called her Ha-Ha, and she was very proud of the name.

It is ironic that my mother suffered depression many times during her life. But she is remembered as Ha-Ha, which always brings to mind the happy times that we shared with her.

Ease

My first grandson named me Ease. It, of course, is short for Louise.

I had a hard time believing that I was going to be a grandmother. It was difficult to think that I was old enough. And harder still to believe that I was wise enough—as wise as grandmothers are supposed to be. I felt that the transition from mother to grandmother would be a difficult one.

But when my grandson called me Ease for the first time, I knew that everything I had conjured up about my shortcomings was wrong. I actually made the transition with "ease." Do you know why? Because that grandson of mine is so "easy" to love. And when everything is said and done—love is all you really need anyway, right?

The one thing we never give enough of is love.

—Henry Miller

I love my grandmother because she has a good shoulder to cry on.

If I'd known grandchildren were going to be so much fun, I'd have had them first.

—Anonymous

There is a first for everything—
but nothing compares to becoming a
grandparent for the first time!

LITTLE EYES UPON YOU

There are little eyes upon you
And they're watching night and day.
There are little ears that quickly
Take in every word you say.
There are little hands all eager
To do anything you do;
And a little boy who's dreaming
Of the day he'll be like you.
You're the little fellow's idol,
You're the wisest of the wise.
In his little mind about you
No suspicions ever rise.
He believes in you devoutly,
Holds all you say and do;

He will say and do, in your way
When he's grown up just like you.
There's a wide-eyed little fellow
Who believes you're always right;
And his eyes are always opened,
And he watches day and night.
You are setting an example
Every day in all you do;
For the little boy who's waiting
To grow up to be like you.

—Anonymous

My son, age four, looked at my
mother the other day and said,
"Gram, are you getting old?" "No!"
she replied quickly. "I'm not getting
older. I'm just getting happier."
She smiled and winked at him.

Age is of no importance unless you are a cheese.

—Billie Burke

As my grandfather always said:

Play dead if a bear is coming.

If you see a good-looking girl, ask her out.

Cool Pop

Josh's step-grandfather had no children of his own. When he married Josh's grandmother, he inherited an entire family, and he was very excited. He took to Josh with all the fervor of a true, blooded grandfather. He and Josh go fishing and play ball, and he makes special phone calls to Josh just to see how school is going and how he is doing.

Whenever Josh visits, his step-grandfather always has Josh's favorite treat waiting for him—a frozen ice cool-pop. From that came the perfect name for the coolest grandfather—Cool Pop!

My grandparents are sweet and easy. She is Sweet and he is Easy—and that's what I call them!

—Lannie Jewell

Easy

Isn't it funny how we evolve as we grow older? Most young men would never want to be known as Easy. But that is how my father is known to his grandchildren, and he is very proud.

His last name is Eslick. Now, this name lends itself to several nicknames, but my father chose Easy as his grandfather name. My mother, on the other hand, had always liked the name Old Sweet for her grandmother name. When my children and my nephew came along they began calling my mother and father Sweet and Easy. What wonderful, appropriate names for them! They are integral parts of their grandchildren's lives, and they definitely live up to their names.

The simplest toy, one which even the youngest child can operate, is called a grandparent.

—Sam Levenson

My grandmother is a role model to me. Sometimes I will catch myself telling her about different feelings that I have or changes that I am going through. Just by the way she looks at me, I can see that she has been there before. She has been down these roads . . . I see her, and I see her experiences. She is kind and loving. I long for my experiences to teach me to be the type of woman that she is.

Grand Micki

This cool grandmother has a Volkswagen convertible named Minnie, a tattooed Minnie Mouse on her ankle, and the Disney store is an automatic stop on shopping trips with her grandchildren. Mickey Mouse is their favorite Disney character.

Micki is her name! Her grandchildren call her Grand Micki. She loves it and hopes they will remember her as a very fun and lovable character, just as they think of the well-known mouse.

I love my grandmother because every Sunday she
took me to buy ice cream!

I love my grandmother because when I married,
she created a special cookbook with
all of her best recipes for me.

Ibo

In my husband's very small hometown, whenever you made a phone call, you would pick up the receiver and ask the operator to connect you to the number. When my husband's sister, Susan, was a little girl, she called her grandmother Ibo. This was short for Isabelle, which Susan could not pronounce.

Well, word must have traveled about Ibo's name. One day when Susan was still too young to use the phone, she picked it up and the operator asked her for the number.

"I want to talk to Ibo," Susan replied. As luck would have it, the operator knew just whom she was talking about and put the call right through. How surprised was Ibo when she heard her young granddaughter's voice on the other line. And how we all wish we could call her now.

I LOVE MY *Grandmother* BECAUSE . . .

She taught me to fold napkins and set the table.

∽

She comes to my school to eat lunch with me.

She encourages me to do my best
and try to make the honor roll.

∞

She buys anything that I have to sell for school.

∞

She asks her friends to order Girl Scout cookies
from me.

I LOVE MY *Grandfather* BECAUSE . . .

We collect baseball cards together.

∞

We watch old Western movies together.

We go to ball games. We don't sit; we walk the fence!

He wrote me encouraging notes when I was in college.

He's a doctor, so if I get hurt, he knows what to do!

Your grandchildren are the most beautiful leaves on the family tree.

Daddy Doc

We had the choice of calling my grandfather Daddy Horace or Daddy Melvin, because his name is Horace Melvin.

In a town as small as half a minute and with as many animals as humans, my grandfather was the makeshift veterinarian. Whenever a pig lost its squeal or a chicken was cooped up, the neighbors called on "Doc" Copley. Daddy Doc probably delivered more calves and colts than a real vet could ever imagine—and all without a lick of schooling. He also had his own homemade anesthetic!

So when it came time to choose a name for him, instead of Daddy Horace or Daddy Melvin, we called him Daddy Doc. For some reason, he preferred that over Horace or Melvin.

Dat

When my daughter was born, my father, who lives in another state, jumped on a plane and arrived in time to be one of the first persons to hold her. He stayed through the week and rarely moved from the rocking chair in the den, where he held his new granddaughter and sang to her for hours.

After he left, I worried that the distance between our homes would make it difficult for him to have a close relationship with our little Lauren. We visited him twice during her first year, and then I became pregnant with my second child, making it difficult for us to make the long trip.

Lauren was nineteen months old before my father was able to come and visit us again. Enthusiastically, I told her again and again that her grandfather was coming to visit, hoping she would love him as I do. When he arrived, Lauren greeted him as if she knew quite well that this was a special person in her life. We went out to eat dinner, and she sat next to him, studying him closely.

Back at home, it was Lauren's bedtime. I asked her to tell her granddad good night. She walked over to him on her way to her room, stopped in front of him, and stood silently for a few seconds. She then gave a big smile and a wave and said, "Bye Dat!" So, "Dat was Dat," as they say. Theirs has been a close, loving special relationship despite my worries about the long distance between them.

I love my grandfather because he helped coach our Little League team.

Nobody can do for little children what grandparents do. Grandparents sort of sprinkle stardust over the lives of little children.

—Alex Haley

Graduate. Go on to college.
Never, never stop learning good things.

If it sounds too good to be true, it probably is.

Great Ways to Help Your Grandchild Remember You

- Videotape yourself reading a book, telling funny stories, or even talking about your family history.

- Coach a Little League Team.

- Share with them your favorite author or movie.

- Take a walk, or sit together under a favorite tree and talk.

- Play games with them.

Through my grandfather's eyes I see:
beauty in nature, in people,
and in my grandma;
bravery during the wars that were fought;
honor in the hard work he has done to
support his family and in the life he has led;
love for country, for others, for family,
and for God;
hope for me, my children,
and the generations to come.

My grandmothers are full of memories,
Smelling of soap and onions and wet clay
With veins rolling roughly over quick hands.
They have many clean words to say.
My grandmothers were strong.

Margaret Walker

Cuckoo Nana

I loved to go to my grandmother's house when I was little. We would play and laugh and have so much fun. She had a large cuckoo clock that fascinated me. My mother said that every time it would chime, I would run and watch the bird come out. My grandmother would stand beside me, and together we would announce with "cuckoos" whatever hour it was.

Because I loved the clock so much, whenever I would cry, my grandmother would do a funny face and say, "Cuckoo, Cuckoo," to cheer me up. That's why I call her Cuckoo Nana. She was so funny and always so happy! Now that old cuckoo clock stands in my house, and every time the clock chimes, I remember Cuckoo Nana and look forward to the day when I can hold my own grandchild in front of the clock and tell him or her about my grandmother, my Cuckoo Nana.

I love my grandmother because she wrote me letters while I was at camp telling me how much she missed me and some funny things my grandpa had done while I was away.

Gong Gong

My husband and I lived right down the street from my parents. My mother had her own sales business and was on the go all of the time.

As my daughter grew older, she got into the habit of running to our front window to watch for her grandmother's car to go by. Every morning you could see her little body inside the curtain looking out the window. Pretty soon, I would hear my mother's car horn blowing and I would hear my daughter say, "Gone, gone."

Somehow, "Gone, gone" turned into Gong Gong, and that's a very appropriate name for a grandmother who's always on the run.

Everybody should try to have a grand-
mother, especially if you don't have a TV,
because grandmothers are the only adults
who have time to spare.

Minnie

Mary Ann was a lady of small stature, but the most distinctive quality about her was her voice. She had a small, squeaky voice. In fact, she sounded just like Minnie Mouse.

One day, her oldest grandchild noticed this while watching cartoons. "You sound like Minnie, Grandma!" And from that day on, all the kids called her Minnie.

*I love my grandmother because she's fun
and my friends love her too.*

I love my grandfather because he overlooks my faults and praises my strenghts.

PawPaw

When I was born, my brother was already calling my grandfather PawPaw. My PawPaw has three daughters. I was his first granddaughter, and he really took to me because he loves little girls.

I am very possessive of my PawPaw. He calls me Sugar Baby. When my cousin Caroline was born, I heard him call her Sugar Baby, too. Well, I set him straight! He could only have one Sugar Baby, and that was me! So he decided to call her Sweet Linegirl.

I don't know why we call him PawPaw. It reminds me of the song "Way Down Yonder in the PaPaw Patch." I know if I were in that papaw patch I would definitely pick my PawPaw and put him in my basket. He's the best grandfather in the universe. I love him very much.

Dandy

When my children were very young, our family vacationed in South Florida. In the early evenings before dinner, several older men, all retired and aged seventy-five or so, would gather together to visit and discuss their tennis or golf games. Most of these fellows were well dressed, but one old gent in particular impressed me because he was always impeccably dressed in lime green, canary yellow, or sky blue trousers coordinated with a blazer of equally bright (but contrasting) color as well as matching shirt, socks, etc. He was small and bold and seemed so happy. I never forgot him. Years later, when my wife and I were told we would be first-time grandparents, we were discussing with another couple interesting grandparent names. They told us about a grandfather they knew who was called Dandy. I thought immediately of the happy little dandy in Florida years ago and knew what I wanted to be called. Today my wife and I have six grandchildren whose southern accents have added an extra syllable to my name: Day-Yun-Dy. Music to my ears.

I LOVE MY *Grandfather* BECAUSE . . .

He taught me about the stock market.

◌

He taught me the importance of a good work ethic.

He helped me build my dog house.

He always comes to Grandparents Day at my school.

He takes me on long bike rides.

I LOVE MY *Grandmother* BECAUSE . . .

She will read me my favorite story over and over
and over again.

୦ଠ

She doesn't make me take naps if I don't want to.

She doesn't give me clothes for presents . . . only really cool toys and money!

∞

She e-mails me cool websites and jokes.

∞

She lets me push the buggy in the grocery store.

When the grandmothers of today hear the word "Chippendales," they don't necessarily think of chairs.

—Joan Kerr

Hazelnut

At first, we were a little afraid of our grandmother. My first remembrance of her is when she was in her seventies. She lived in a big Victorian house in a small mining town in Kentucky. There was a Revolutionary War soldier's grave in her yard, and sometimes we would hear the doors rattle in her attic, so we were pretty much convinced that her house was haunted. She stood five feet tall and had a hunchback. Every time we went to her house, she fixed green pea soup and made us eat all of it. My cousins lived with her, and the main thing I remember them telling me was that she "shore could give some whuppins." As little boys, we thought she was crazy. Her name was Hazel, so we called her "Hazelnut"—but we never did it to her face!

A fter winter break a teacher asked her young pupils to write how they spent the holidays. One child wrote the following:

> We always spend the holidays with Grandma and Grandpa. They used to live here in a big brick house, but Grandpa got retarded, and they moved to Florida. Now they live in a place with a lot of other retarded people.
>
> They live in a tin box and have rocks painted green to look like grass. They ride around on big tricycles and wear name tags because they don't know who they are anymore.
>
> They go to a building called a wrecked center, but they must have got it fixed because it is all right now. They play games and do exercises there, but they don't do them very well. There is a swimming pool too, but they all jump

up and down in it with their hats on. I guess they don't know how to swim.

At their gate, there is a doll house with a little old man sitting in it. He watches all day so nobody can escape. Sometimes they sneak out. Then they go cruising in their golf carts.

My grandma used to bake cookies and stuff, but I guess she forgot how. Nobody there cooks; they just eat out. And they eat the same thing every night—Early Birds.

Some of the people can't get past the man in the doll house to go out. So the ones who do get out bring food back to the wrecked center and call it pot luck. My grandma says grandpa worked all his life to earn his retardment and says I should work hard so I can be retarded some day too. When I earn my retardment I want to be the man in the doll house. Then I will let people out!

Mama Bear

She was the divorced mother of two little boys. Then she married a man with a young son, who heard her two boys calling her Mama, and he tried to do the same. But this made his real mama mad.

So she tried to explain to him that he already had a mama, and she was his step-mama. One day she was frustrated trying to explain this to him as he was looking at her collection of dolls and teddy bears, which he loved. "O.K.," he smiled at her and said, "then you are my mama bear!"

This name thrilled her friends. Before she married, she had been a petite 105 pounds, but with her new marital bliss, she had gained sixty pounds. "I do look like a mama bear!" she laughed.

Now all three boys are older and they have children of their own. Mama bear is back down to her small size, has long blonde hair, and looks not a day over thirty. But she is still Mama Bear to her children and grandchildren—a very beautiful Mama Bear, indeed.

${Y}$ou don't have to look like a granny to be one.

—Author Unknown

Grandparents are our continuing tie to the near-past, to the events and beliefs and experiences that so strongly affect our lives and the world around us. Whether they are our own or surrogate grandparents who fill some of the gaps in our mobile society, our senior generation also provides our society a link to our national heritage and traditions.

We all know grandparents whose values transcend passing fads and pressures and who possess the wisdom of distilled pain and joy. Because they are usually free to love and guide and befriend the young without having to take daily responsibility for them, they can often reach out past pride and fear of failure and close the space between generations."

—Jimmy Carter

I love my grandfather because he loves my grandmother.

The authors extend their sincere gratitude to the following individuals who contributed to this book. (Stories were edited for clarity and style.)

Amy Baughman	Bryan Curtis	Cindy Fowler
Holly Baulch	Patsy Curtis	Kari Lou Frank
Joyce Blaylock	Karen Davies	Cathy Fridge
Lemelia Bonner	Sandy Davis	Calvert Garstin
Jim Bradford	Angela Dixon	Donna Gillentine
Jackie Brown	Alan Dooley	Adonis Gordon
Beth Burress	Vicki Dooley	Lisa Gorman
Taylor Cawley	Lynn Dorris	Marsha Griffin
Virginia Cheek	Allison Dowsley	Mary Griffin
Sheila Clark	Barrettt Dozier	Walter Griffin
Karmen Clift	Lois Ellis	Mary Hargis
Tressa Copley	Luanna Elrod	Sue Hayes
Beth Corcoran	Betty Eskew	Mark Henderson
Cara Crews	Ashley Evans	Edward Henderson
Carolyn Culpepper	Darlene Evans	Becky Henry

Carrie Henry
Tracy Henry
Chris Hodge
Dee Ann Hodge
Freddy Hodge
Barbara Hubbard
Nancy Huddleston
Sally Hudgins
Sandy Hudson
Beth Hutcheson
Montez Jenkins
Lannie Jewell
Martha Johnson
Nan Jorgensen
Sherri Kale
Pat Kepler
Camille Lowe
Patsy Luckett
Robbie Malone

Neal Matthews
Sydney Myers
Linda O'Neal
Ashleigh Orme
Lanell Padgett
Johnny Padgett
Battle Page
Gina Page
Peggy Parker
Tammy Parker
Thomas Parker
Olene Patterson
Andra Patton
Micki Pendleton
Donna Phillips
Elizabeth Puryear
Marinda Rice
Bob Richter
Angie Ryan

Teresa (Wendler) Sav
Embry Savage
Susan Schultz
Jonathan Seyfred
Genevieve Smith
Mary Stapleton
Kathy Steakley
William Stevenson
Lisa Stinson
Jamie Stofka
Clara Ruth Stone
LeAnne Terry
Tim Terry
Keith Thetford
Julia Webb
Glenda Whitaker
Benja Whitelaw
Sharon Winter
Jo Wright